PENGUIN BOOKS

SIIMON REYNOLDS is one of the most well-known and respected names in advertising. He has won almost every major advertising award for creativity in the world, including the Gold Lion at Cannes, the Gold Pencil at the New York One Show and the Grand Prize at the London International Advertising Festival. In Australia he has won Newspaper Ad of the Year, TV Commercial of the Year, Magazine Ad of the Year and Advertising Agency of the Year (twice).

Siimon is a winner of the International Advertising Association Scholarship and NSW Young Career Achiever of the Year. He has lectured nationally on advertising to over 50 000 businesspeople, and is a successful author in six countries. He is now Creative Director of Love, an advertising, PR and brand-building company, and co-founder of the Photon Group, a consortium of 13 marketing companies, which recently listed on the Australian Stock Exchange.

better than chocolate

50 proven ways to feel happier

Siimon Reynolds

PENGUIN BOOKS

PENGUIN BOOKS

Published by the Penguin Group
Penguin Group (Australia)
250 Camberwell Road
Camberwell, Victoria 3124, Australia
(a division of Pearson Australia Group Pty Ltd)
Penguin Group (USA) Inc.
375 Hudson Street, New York, New York 10014, USA
Penguin Group (Canada)
10 Alcorn Avenue, Toronto, Ontario, Canada, M4V 3B2
(a division of Pearson Penguin Canada Inc.)
Penguin Books Ltd
80 Strand, London WC2R 0RL, England
Penguin Ireland
25 St Stephen's Green, Dublin 2, Ireland
(a division of Penguin Books Ltd)
Penguin Books India Pvt Ltd
11, Community Centre, Panchsheel Park, New Delhi-110 017, India
Penguin Group (NZ)
Cnr Airborne and Rosedale Roads, Albany, Auckland, New Zealand
(a division of Pearson New Zealand Ltd)
Penguin Books (South Africa) (Pty) Ltd
24 Sturdee Avenue, Rosebank, Johannesburg 2196, South Africa

Penguin Books Ltd, Registered Offices: 80 Strand, London WC2R 0RL, England

First published by Penguin Group (Australia), a division of Pearson Australia Group Pty Ltd, 2004

10 9 8 7 6 5 4 3 2 1

Text copyright © Siimon Reynolds 2004
Illustrations copyright © John Canty 2004

The moral right of the author has been asserted

Designed and illustrated by John Canty © Penguin Group (Australia)
Typeset in 9.5/18 Scala Sans by Post Pre-press Group, Brisbane, Queensland
Printed and bound in Australia by McPherson's Printing Group, Maryborough, Victoria

National Library of Australia
Cataloguing-in-Publication data:

Reynolds, Siimon.
Better than chocolate : 50 proven ways to feel happier.

Bibliography.
ISBN 0 14 300296 1.

1. Happiness. 2. Self-actualization (Psychology). I. Title.

158.1

www.penguin.com.au

To Kath,
source of so much happiness

CONTENTS INTRODUCTION viii   MAKE A HAPPINESS LIST 1

EXERCISE 3   TRY COGNITIVE THERAPY 5   GET IN FLOW 7

DEVELOP THE MAGIC FOUR PERSONALITY CHARACTERISTICS 9

MEDITATE 11 DON'T STRESS ABOUT MONEY 13 UNDERSTAND

THE BUDDHIST THEORY 15   TRY A LOW-INSULIN DIET 17

TAKE CONTROL 19 ASK UPLIFTING QUESTIONS 21 DEVELOP

DISCIPLINE 23 REMEMBER GOD 25 INCREASE FRIENDSHIPS 27

GET MARRIED 29 CLARIFY YOUR VALUES 31 BE GRATEFUL 33

BALANCE YOUR HORMONES 35 CHANGE YOUR BREATHING 37

DEVELOP FUTURE FOCUS 39   FOLLOW THE TAOIST WAY 41

INCREASE OMEGA-3 43 SET CLEAR GOALS 45 RELEASE YOUR

ENERGY 47 ACT HAPPY 49 INCREASE SLEEP 51 WORK ON

YOUR SELF-IMAGE 53 CHANGE FOCUS 55 BE AN OPTIMIST 57

CARE FOR OTHERS 59   LAUGH 61   PRACTISE RELIGION 63

TAKE MASSIVE ACTION 65   SEEK INTERNAL GOALS 67

SIMPLIFY YOUR LIFE 69   CREATE A LIFE PURPOSE 71

BECOME A SELF-ACTUALISER 73   GET BUSY 75   LIVE BY THE

CONFUCIAN THEORY 77   SMILE 79   GET SOME SUNLIGHT 81

POLISH YOUR MEMORIES 83   FORGIVE 85   PRACTISE LOVING-

KINDNESS 87   FIND SATISFYING WORK 89   LIMIT TIME

ALONE 91   PLAN AND PRIORITISE 93   REDUCE ALCOHOL 95

TAKE L-TYROSINE 97   LISTEN TO UPBEAT MUSIC 99   USE

POSITIVE AFFIRMATIONS 101   EXPRESS YOUR LOVE 103   MEET

NEW PEOPLE 105   TURN OFF THE TV 107   VOLUNTEER 109

CHOOSE THE BRIGHT SIDE 111   LOOK FORWARD TO THE

FUTURE 113   HAVE MORE CONVERSATIONS 115   DRESS

SEXILY 117   BOOK HOLIDAYS IN ADVANCE 119   GET A PET 121

CREATE AN ACTIVITY GROUP 123   BE A FILMGOER 125   KISS

SOMEONE 127   FOLLOW A TEAM 129   BE SENSITIVE 131

FOCUS ON HAPPINESS 133   RECOMMENDED READING 134

INTRODUCTION   Happiness is not an accident. There are numerous simple techniques anyone can use to help them live a more joyful life. Only trouble is, very few people know about them.

That's because the field of 'Positive Psychology', or how to be happy, is one of the newest areas of science, and news of its discoveries has not yet reached the general population. With the publication of this book, that is about to change.

This guide may be small, but it contains a summary of all the major contemporary theories on happiness. I have deliberately kept it brief to enable you to grasp the keys to increasing your bliss without having to wade through mountains of scientific research.

These techniques have all been tested, many under rigorous clinical conditions. They're proven to be not just effective, but life-changing. I do hope you enjoy *Better than Chocolate*.

More importantly, I hope you'll try to make the techniques and principles a part of your life. After all, there is surely no more important issue in our lives than our happiness.

Happy reading.

Things that make me happy

1

2

3

4

5

If you're feeling listless,

make a list

MAKE A HAPPINESS LIST When I first heard of this technique I was struck by its simplicity. High-performance expert Fred Grosse recommends his students write a list of all the activities they love doing. It could be anything from walking on a beach at sunset to having a long bath.

Then, at the beginning of each week, schedule at least one of these 'moments' in your diary every day. Allocate a specific time for it to ensure you'll make it happen. With this simple system, your life soon becomes filled with many more enjoyable, happy moments. Just as important, this technique forces you to be more conscious of your happiness and to make it a top priority.

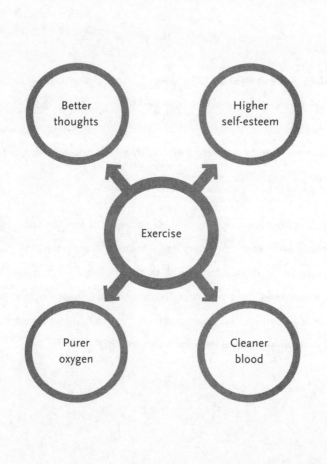

EXERCISE   Daily exercise can have a huge impact on how positive we feel. There are several reasons why. First, giving our body a regular work-out helps reduce tension and stress. Second, studies have shown that exercise changes our body's biochemistry. During exercise we produce natural opiates, known as endorphins, that make us feel happier – hence the famous 'runner's high'.

Finally, regular exercise reduces fat, improves muscle tone, clears the skin and makes us feel strong. These changes often lead to a significant increase in self-esteem, a mental state closely linked with happiness.

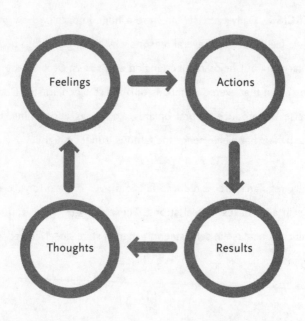

TRY COGNITIVE THERAPY   In the last 20 years, mainstream psychology has taken an enormous leap forward. Where once Freud and Jung claimed that emotions affect our thinking, today's cognitive therapists emphasise that thinking also alters our moods. To feel happier, they say, we must direct our thinking.

When you next feel down, try this simple but powerful cognitive therapy technique:

1. Write down what you are thinking.
2. Question this on paper – is the thought helpful and realistic?
3. Write down a more positive way of looking at your situation.

Try it now. You'll be surprised at how this elementary cognitive process can work wonders.

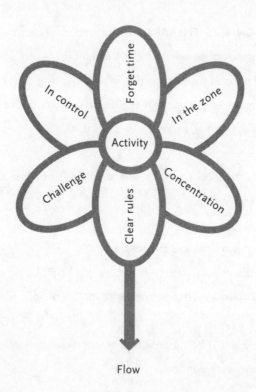

Flow

GET IN FLOW   Flow theory is one of the most important break-throughs of the last 20 years. Mihaly Csikszentmihalyi, its pioneer, suggests that enjoyment consists of four components:

1. we are doing an activity that is challenging
2. it is clear how we are progressing (the rules are simple)
3. it takes all our concentration
4. but we are making progress and feel in control.

We tend to experience flow when we practise a discipline such as an art, a sport or a religion. (Activities such as watching TV are not usually flowful because they lack a sense of achievement.) The more flow activities we incorporate into our lives, the happier we feel. What five activities create flow for you, and how could you do more of them each week?

Happy individuals share
four characteristics

DEVELOP THE MAGIC FOUR PERSONALITY CHARACTERISTICS

According to the research of David Myers (a leading Positive Psychology therapist), people who tend to be happier than the average exhibit four characteristics:

1. high self-esteem
2. a feeling of control over life
3. optimism
4. extroversion (surprising but true).

To the degree that we can increase these personality traits, our happiness levels will usually rise. Take a few minutes now to write down one way you could cultivate these four traits in your own character.

Meditation clears your mind

MEDITATE Twenty years of research by Herbert Benson of Harvard Medical School shows that people who meditate regularly are usually happier than those who don't. Not sure how to meditate? He suggests this straightforward technique:

1. Choose a simple word, e.g. calm, love, one, or peace.
2. Repeat that word to yourself for 10 to 20 minutes. You can either say the word aloud or just hear it in your mind, every second or two.
3. Disregard everyday thoughts that come up and return to your repetition.

It's that easy. And that hard!

If you focus on money
happiness goes down

DON'T STRESS ABOUT MONEY In today's society, there is an ever-increasing array of stuff we are tempted to buy. New furniture. The latest electronics. This season's must-have dress. That hot new car. The list goes on. But it's all a trap. Growing scientific research shows that an obsession with material gain actually makes us less happy. Positive Psychology expert Martin Seligman has shown that those who focus purely on making more money are less happy than the average person.

What's more, it has been proven that once someone's income rises above the basic poverty line, there is little difference in happiness between them and the rich. Studies indicate that the availability of material possessions is nine times less vital to happiness than personal assets like friends and family. Clearly, the old adage is true: money really does not make you happy.

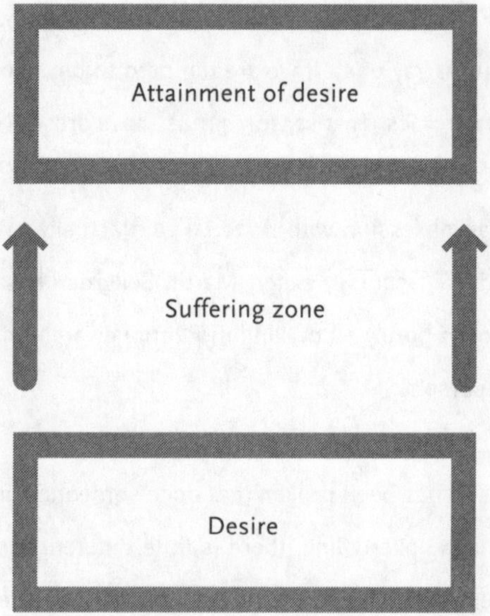
Attainment of desire
Suffering zone
Desire

UNDERSTAND THE BUDDHIST THEORY The classical Buddhist theory on happiness centres on desire. Buddhists believe that reducing our desires and cravings is a sure path to feeling happy. It is desire, they say, that is the cause of much of our frustration and misery. There are two simple ways to minimise desire:

1. achieve what we desire
2. reduce our desires.

Buddhists suggest that the first is extremely difficult to achieve and that the second offers a quicker road to bliss. Of course, for the average person, it doesn't make sense to have no desires at all. Where would the fun be in life? But ask yourself, 'Would I be happier if I reduced the number of things I want?' The answer may surprise you.

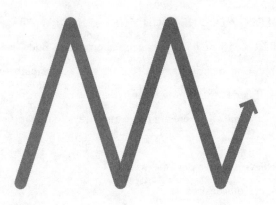

Changing sugar levels change mood

TRY A LOW-INSULIN DIET Building on the work of the controversial Robert Atkins, of the 'Atkins Diet' fame, Barry Sears has shown that the typical western diet – high in sugars and grains – plays havoc with our hormone balances, and therefore our emotions. As blood sugar levels vary greatly with every meal, we experience regular mood swings.

Sears' solution, known as the Zone Diet, is to blend meat or fish with vegetables (excluding potato, pumpkin and other simple root vegetables) and to balance sugar levels with a piece of fruit every four hours. This diet not only stabilises our moods, it helps many to lose weight. Many Zone Dieters also report they are more mentally focused and experience a significant increase in energy levels.

Happiness is linked
to perceived Control

TAKE CONTROL A common characteristic of happy people is that they feel they have control over their lives. If you are unhappy, review your life to see where you feel things are out of control. Then take action.

Write a list of all the areas in your life where you feel you don't have control. Now write down three things you could do to improve each situation. Perhaps you need to tell someone how you really feel. Maybe you need to change direction, or let something (or someone) go. Taking action can be hard, but if the result increases your sense of control over your life, you are likely to feel much happier for it.

Questions can change the
direction of your thinking

ASK UPLIFTING QUESTIONS The mind can easily be 'guided' towards thinking happy thoughts with the use of simple questions. Regularly asking ourselves the following questions can have a noted effect on our life satisfaction:

1. What am I happy about in my life?
2. What is going well?
3. What am I excited about?
4. What can I look forward to?

For best results, ask yourself these questions each morning and at the end of the day. Be sure to take a few minutes to dwell on the pleasant and inspiring answers.

Discipline increases happiness

DEVELOP DISCIPLINE According to the spiritualist Shaykh Fadhlalla Haeri, one of the essential factors in a person's happiness is their level of self-discipline. Regular overindulgence in food, alcohol, sex, even thinking can tax and weaken our body, mind and soul.

Practising self-discipline in these areas strengthens our mind and self-image, as we begin to see ourselves as master of our body, rather than its slave. Restraint leads to stability; stability to content-ment. Take a few moments to evaluate your life. In what areas do you lack self-discipline? What are three simple things you could do to tame those weaknesses?

1000

This happiness technique has been
used for over one thousand years

REMEMBER GOD This happiness technique has been used by Muslims, Jews and followers of some branches of Christianity for thousands of years with reputedly outstanding success. As you go about your day, try to remember constantly that God is with you, in you and all around you. Or if you are not religious, you can remember Nature, the source of all that we are.

Practitioners say that reminding ourselves that there is a loving Creator who is 'running the show' calms us, comforts us and gives us faith that we can overcome life's temporary but often disturbing setbacks. Remembering God throughout the day also helps centre us, and stops us getting too wrapped up in the daily challenges life continues to throw at us.

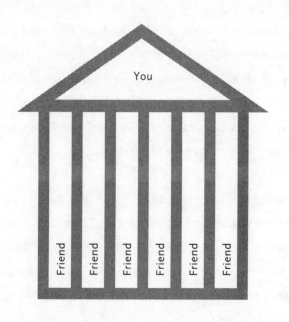

Friends make you feel supported

INCREASE FRIENDSHIPS   There is a strong connection between how many good friends we have and how happy we tend to be. Studies show that those of us with five or more good friends often reach higher levels of happiness than those with fewer pals.

Happiness researcher Ed Diener has shown that the happiest people have both more close and more casual friends than the average person. Write a list of ten people whose company you enjoy. How could you improve your relationship with them? What could you do to bring them more into your world?

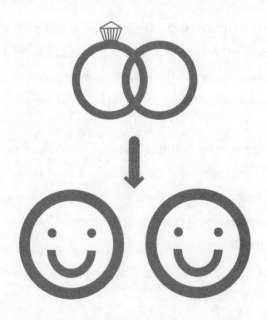

Married couples
are usually happier

GET MARRIED   With all the talk of rising divorce rates, marriage has received a hard rap in recent times. However, growing research indicates that married people are generally happier than those who are single.

The National Opinion Research Center carried out a major survey of around 35 000 Americans over the last 30 years. Around 40% of married people suggested they were very happy versus 24% of single people (including those who were divorced, widowed or separated). Marriage may have its ups and downs, but for most people there are more ups.

Cloudy thinking can
lead to unhappiness

CLARIFY YOUR VALUES   Most people are happy or miserable not because of particular events but because of how they react to them. If we are living our life according to our values, we tend to feel happy. If we aren't, we're less likely to feel happy. Only trouble is, most people are not clear on what they value in life.

Try this quick test. Prioritise the following five values in order of importance in your life: health, career, family, spirituality, social life. Now ask yourself, 'Do I live my life according to these priorities?' If not, perhaps it's time you did. Spending time choosing values to live by can be an invaluable step in simplifying your life and increasing your bliss.

Gratitude

Happiness

BE GRATEFUL   This is one of the simplest happiness techniques, but also one of the most powerful. Dan Sullivan, a renowned expert in human potential, points out that it is virtually impossible to experience negative emotions when we are feeling grateful.

Because we tend to feel up or down according to what we're focusing on, a few minutes each day sitting in quiet gratitude can work wonders on our happiness level. From my own experience, I believe that constantly expressing and feeling gratitude is one of the surest ways to a lastingly happy life. What could you be grateful for?

Hormones need to be balanced

BALANCE YOUR HORMONES Human Growth Hormone (HGH) is thought by many longevity scientists to be one of the primary rebuilders of the human being. It is in many ways the fountain of youth. But after age 30, our ability to produce HGH declines by about 10% a decade. Regular top-ups of HGH have been shown to give older people back their vitality, significantly improve their optimism and balance their moods.

If you are over 50, ask your doctor how HGH can help you feel better and stronger. Or contact a longevity expert for a comprehensive analysis of how natural hormonal treatments can make you happier and healthier. And as this is a new treatment, don't forget to research the potential side effects as well.

2

Oxygen intake is linked to mood

CHANGE YOUR BREATHING   Every time we get angry, our breathing changes. Every time we are blissed out, it has a different pattern again. Clearly, our moods affect our breathing. But research has revealed it works the other way as well. If we breathe in deeply, and in a totally relaxed way, it's almost impossible to remain angry or frustrated. Deep breathing creates a calmer, more relaxed and happy person.

Next time you are angry or down, try it for yourself. Consciously alter your breathing pattern. Breathe deeper, slower. In through the nose and out through the mouth. Within minutes you'll find your bad mood dissolving.

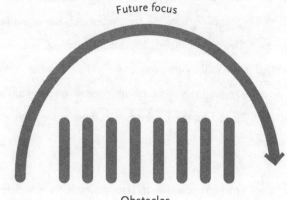

Future focus

Obstacles

DEVELOP FUTURE FOCUS   Most people have no real vision for their future. As a result, they often get caught up in day-to-day troubles. Having a future focus not only makes life more exciting, it helps make any short-term problems more bearable.

To experience a fundamentally happier life, decide where you would like to be in 10 years and work towards it daily. See it clearly, believe in it. Take action to make it a reality. Take out a pen and some paper. Imagine your ideal life in a decade. Where would you live? How would you work? What would you have achieved? It's almost impossible to feel depressed if you have a strong future focus that you work towards with hope and consistency every day.

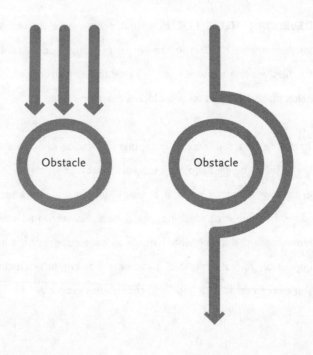

Typical human way   A river's way

FOLLOW THE TAOIST WAY Taoism, along with Buddhism and Confucianism, is one of the three great philosophical schools of ancient China. Although not so many of us have heard of this philosophy, the *Tao Te Ching* – the main text of Taoism – is the most translated work in the world, other than the Bible.

Taoists believe that happiness can be obtained by following nature. For instance, water always travels around rocks, so we should try to go around problems rather than plough directly through them. When a tiger's belly is full, it stops hunting – in the same way, we should not work constantly or take more than we need. You get the picture.

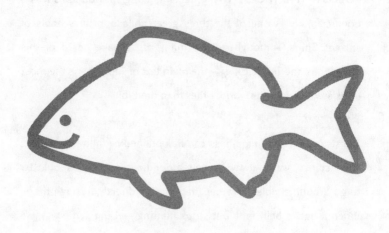

Omega-3 lifts mood.

Ever seen an unhappy fish?

INCREASE OMEGA-3   Our diet is intricately linked to our mental state. According to Andrew Stoll of Harvard Medical School, a lack of omega-3 fats in our diet is one reason why so many people feel depressed. Stoll says study after study has shown that consuming more omega-3 helps reduce the symptoms of depression and schizophrenia, and increase happy moods.

So, how do you get more omega-3? It's easy. Just eat more deep-sea fish like salmon or tuna. Or pick up some omega-3 supplements from your pharmacist or health-food store.

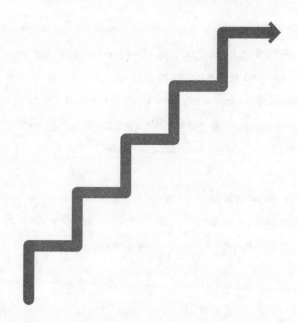

Exciting goals provide direction

SET CLEAR GOALS   Our brains are goal-activating mechanisms. We tell our brain what we want and it devises a system for getting there. The problem, according to achievement expert Brian Tracy, is that only around 3% of the population set goals. No wonder so many people feel that their life has little or no direction.

It's easily remedied though. Grab a piece of paper now and spend 10 minutes dreaming about what you would like to achieve in the following areas: health, career, social, family, spiritual, pleasure. Then choose your five favourite goals and begin acting – today – to make them happen. You'll find each step you take towards your goals will increase both your self-esteem and your wellbeing.

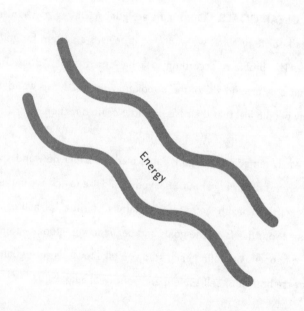

Energy

Energy flows through
rivers called meridians

RELEASE YOUR ENERGY Both the Indian yoga experts and the Chinese tai chi masters agree: smooth energy flow is vital for physical and mental happiness. Our bodies contain rivers of energy, known as meridians. When these are blocked we tend to feel down in the dumps.

But we don't have to spend hours in the lotus position or become kung-fu experts to improve the situation. Spending 10 minutes a day stretching your major limbs and muscles helps unblock these meridians, encouraging the body's energy (*chi* in Mandarin or *prana* in Sanskrit) to circulate freely, improving both your health and your mood.

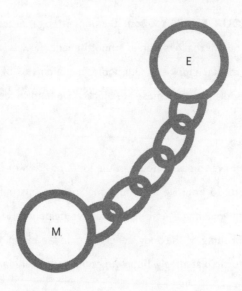

Motion is linked to emotion

ACT HAPPY One of the most effective happiness-inducing techniques is simply to act like you are happy. That's right – just pretend you're in a movie, playing the part of a happy person. Within minutes of pretending, most people report that their bad mood begins to fall away.

According to the legendary NLP (neurolinguistic programming) therapists Grindler and Bandler, the reason is connected to how body movements affect thinking patterns. They discovered that if you move like you are happy (stop slouching, don't drop your head, and so on) you begin to think happy thoughts. Amazing, but true. As Grindler and Bandler put it, motion creates emotion.

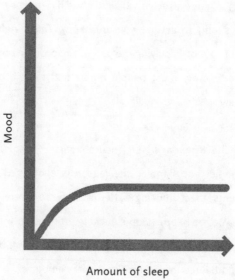

Mood

Amount of sleep

INCREASE SLEEP   In today's society many of us simply do not get enough sleep. A regular shortage of sleep not only makes us physically tired, it also lowers mood and increases irritability, according to sleep therapist and happiness psychologist Timothy Sharp.

Ideal sleep amounts vary from person to person, but usually any amount less than six hours is detrimental to our mood and our body's repair systems. Most people need seven to eight hours sleep per night. If you have trouble sleeping, try eating earlier in the evening, meditating or having a soothing bath before you hit the sack.

As you see yourself
you become

WORK ON YOUR SELF-IMAGE   Plastic surgeon Maxwell Maltz, in his pioneering work *Psycho-Cybernetics*, showed that we usually behave in accordance with the image we have of ourselves. Over time he noticed that the most important factor in a person's happiness was not what they actually looked like, but their self-image. For example, if you view yourself as an unhappy person, your brain will make sure you experience life in accordance with that.

But Maltz showed that our self-image can be re-sculpted, little by little. By visualising yourself being happy for a few minutes each day (literally watching a movie of yourself in your mind), you can improve your levels of life satisfaction significantly.

You can choose what to focus on in life

CHANGE FOCUS Popularised by high-performance coach Anthony Robbins, the Focus Control method of happiness shows quick and powerful results. Robbins argues that we are happy or unhappy largely because of what we focus on. By consciously choosing to focus on what is going well in our life, rather than what may be going poorly, we tend to remain in a buoyant mood.

It's simple to do. Just make a list of five things going well in your life and remind yourself of them several times throughout the day. Within a few days, you'll find your perceptions of the quality of your life will change for the better.

Positive thoughts
add energy

Negative thoughts
subtract energy

BE AN OPTIMIST   Martin Seligman's pioneering work has shown that thinking optimistically is a highly effective way to increase well-being. Seligman has shown that optimistic people:

- are more successful at work
- experience more life enjoyment
- are healthier
- have more friends.

Primarily because they see problems as temporary and don't take them personally, optimists have life enjoyment levels far higher than pessimistic people. What about you? What current problems could you think more positively about?

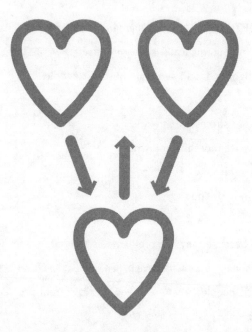

Send love out and you'll
get more love back

CARE FOR OTHERS   Many people who are unhappy are too wrapped up in their own lives. The esteemed psychologist and Sufi spiritual master Javad Nurbakhsh believes unhappy people often feel better if they take the focus away from themselves and focus instead on how others are doing.

Think about it. Could it be that you are a little too self-obsessed? Could over-thinking your situation be the cause of your distress? Resolve to focus on helping other people. Caring for others not only helps you forget your own problems, it can be a hugely uplifting experience in itself.

ha

Laughter lifts your mood

LAUGH This may seem a simplistic antidote to unhappiness, but there is plenty of evidence to support it as an effective one. A classic case study on the effects of humour on wellbeing was written by Norman Cousins in his book *Anatomy of an Illness*.

Cousins suffered from a rare degenerative disease that he cured himself, using a most unusual treatment. He watched comedies on TV for hours, read funny books and spent loads of time laughing each day. Within months he was completely cured. A true story. And a great reminder of the healing power of laughter, even if it is systematically arranged.

God

People who believe in God
are often happier

PRACTISE RELIGION Those who actively practise a religion are often happier than those who do not. What's more, research shows they get divorced less, keep their jobs longer and are usually healthier than their non-religious counterparts.

Many psychologists believe people's faith in a loving deity also inspires them to worry less. As they expect they'll be looked after, their general life contentment increases. Interestingly, those who practise their religion as part of a group experience more of these benefits than those who practise alone.

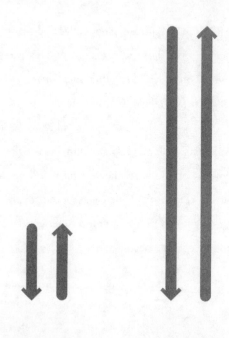

Little actions
Little results

Big actions
Big results

TAKE MASSIVE ACTION If you are suffering because of a particular situation, this could be the perfect technique for you. Too often, when we find ourselves in a difficult position, we withdraw and lick our wounds. That's okay for a while, but taking massive, concerted action to solve the problem usually does more good.

Write a list of 10 ways you could improve the situation, then take action on all 10 today. You may find it challenging to get through all the action steps but if you do, you're likely to see your situation improve radically, in a very short space of time. Whether it's calling a friend, apologising, forgiving, cutting your ties, or whatever, resolve to act powerfully and persistently and you're likely to feel much happier within days.

The key to happiness
is inside your head

SEEK INTERNAL GOALS   You can set yourself two types of goals:

1. internal (quality relationships, wellbeing, personal growth . . .)
2. external (money, power, fame . . .).

Each is worthwhile, but research by Kasser and Ryan, professors of psychology, has shown that the more you develop yourself internally, the happier you will usually be. After interviewing hundreds of people and examining their life priorities, Kasser and Ryan concluded: 'In sum, the pursuit of personal goals for money, fame and attractiveness is shown to lead to a lower quality of life than the goals of relatedness, self-acceptance and community feeling.'

Take a look at your goals. Will they genuinely develop you as a person or will they merely change your outward circumstances?

Juggling too much
can mean discontentment

SIMPLIFY YOUR LIFE   Modern life has become ridiculously busy and complex. By doing less, owning less, worrying less and pushing ourselves less, we can often restore a sense of balance and contentment to our lives. If the complexity of your life is making you unhappy, try these life simplifiers:

- throw out the third of your clothes, books and possessions you do not absolutely need
- reduce your daily work hours by 10%
- schedule three nights a week when you do nothing social
- see less of the friends or family who exhaust you
- spend 20 minutes a day sitting on a sofa doing nothing.

Follow these steps and you'll find that within weeks you're more organised, less tired and considerably happier.

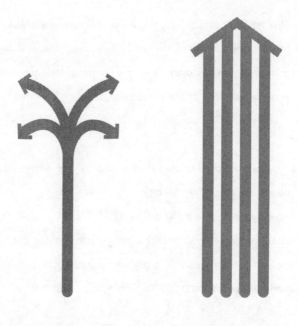

No purpose   Purpose

CREATE A LIFE PURPOSE In his classic book *Man's Search for Meaning*, psychologist Victor Frankl showed that prisoners in Nazi concentration camps during World War II who wanted to survive *for a particular reason* often lived longer than prisoners who had no concrete goal.

Purpose or meaning in our lives is crucial. In fact, many happiness experts believe a sense of meaning or purpose is the attribute most strongly associated with life satisfaction. Frankl even created a new type of psychology – known as Logotherapy – based around this theory.

Why are you alive? Develop a life mission statement – a simple paragraph that sums up your main aim in life. Post it up in your home and workplace, and work towards it daily. As you get clearer about, and more committed to, your life mission, your level of life satisfaction will rise.

Self-actualiser

Self-acceptance

Loving relationships

Freedom from conformity

Clear life purpose

BECOME A SELF-ACTUALISER   Several decades ago, Abraham Maslow became famous in psychology circles with his theory of Self-Actualisation. In order to feel that all our needs are being met, Maslow believed that we need to find our 'calling'. He claimed that, to be lastingly happy, we need the opportunity to unlock our inner potential.

According to Maslow, self-actualisers have developed a wide range of abilities, including:

- self-acceptance
- the ability to maintain loving relationships
- freedom from social pressures and conformity
- a clear sense of purpose and meaning in life.

Which of these could you work on to enhance your life satisfaction?

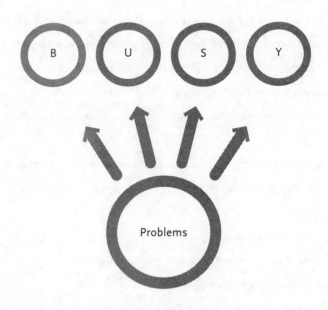

Doing multiple activities
keeps your mind off problems

GET BUSY Over the years, I have often seen friends with little to do slipping into a state of mild depression and lethargy. My observation has been backed up by recent research in the field of Positive Psychology. Apparently the brain craves 'ordered consciousness' and is happier when it has a series of challenging tasks to do.

If you are experiencing down times, create a daily 'To Do' list each morning and get busy. When life seems gloomy, the less time you have to think (and think and think) about your situation, the happier you will often be.

disorder

Lack of order
contradicts your natural state

LIVE BY THE CONFUCIAN THEORY   Perhaps the most significant figure in ancient Chinese history, and certainly the most famous,
Confucius developed several powerful ideas about happiness. These
theories are outlined at length in the *Analects*, a collection of notes
written down by Confucius' disciples after his death.

Confucius believed we can all become happy if we live our lives
according to a strong moral code. His code of chivalry included
living an ordered life, showing love to our family, maintaining social
order, being loyal and consciously developing our character.

Confucius pointed out that even the movement of planets follows
an ordered pattern. Therefore, to live a disordered, disorganised life
goes against nature and creates disharmony.

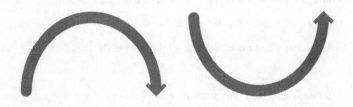

Smiling affects your mood

SMILE   Believe it or not, there has been loads of research on smiling and the power it has to improve a person's mood. Put simply, if you smile you are likely to feel happier.

Researchers Rachel Kettner and Lee-Anne Hather of the University of California studied class photos from a 1961 yearbook of Mills College (a women's college in Oakland). Astonishingly, they found that the women who were smiling broadly and genuinely in the photos were, on average, experiencing significantly more happiness in their lives 30 years later!

Also, let's not forget that smiling at people in your environment tends to put *them* in a better mood too. As the saying goes, smile and the whole world smiles with you.

Sunlight radiates happiness

GET SOME SUNLIGHT   Sunlight can really lift your mood. Conversely, lack of sunlight makes many people feel down. Places like Seattle and Stockholm, where there is little sunlight in winter, report higher suicide rates.

There are two simple ways to remedy the problem. The first is to schedule daily walks in the sun (20 minutes should suffice). The second is to live and work in brightly lit environments. Bright fluorescent light has been shown to have a marked uplifting effect on mood. Full-spectrum lighting (arguably the healthiest artificial light) mimics natural daylight. Although it can be hard to find in stores, there are many full-spectrum lighting retailers online.

You can change your memories
to better support you

POLISH YOUR MEMORIES   Much of the pain we feel in our lives occurs when we remind ourselves of past events. Perhaps we were let down by someone, or we deeply hurt a friend's feelings. Maybe we made a crucially wrong decision or failed in a dramatic and costly way. Whatever our past errors, we can reduce the pain we feel by challenging our memories of them.

Try this exercise. Remember back to one of the events that still causes you pain and see it as a movie in your mind's eye. Now replay the movie, but this time with happy music, at a fast or slow pace, as a black and white film or as a comedy. Replay it again, and again.

If you replay your mind's movie in this new way many times, your brain's recollection of the event will change. It will be virtually impossible to remember that event with the same sadness or pain.

Not forgiving

eats away at your heart

FORGIVE   Every great religion preaches the advantages of genuine forgiveness as a path to happiness. It's easy to see why. Failing to forgive someone eats away at our heart, filling us with anger, envy or hatred every time we think of that person – hardly the ingredients of happiness!

If you are serious about being consistently happy, there is only one thing to do: ring or write to the person in question and let them know you have decided to forgive them. If you do this genuinely, you will feel a huge weight lifted off your shoulders. If they have passed away, write them a letter anyway. Your act of forgiveness will heal and uplift you regardless.

Caring for others
makes you feel good

PRACTISE LOVING-KINDNESS Why do we say, 'It's better to give than to receive'? Because we all know that warm feeling inside when we help someone and lighten their lives. Whether it's a gift, a helping hand or a kind word, showing loving-kindness is one of the quickest and most effective ways to feel good. No one disputes this, but few of us organise our lives to give loving-kindness to those around us.

Think about this for a moment. What if you changed your life purpose from wanting things for yourself to working for others' happiness? Such a fundamental shift could have profound effects on your bliss.

wpolraky

In the best jobs, work and
play are intermingled

FIND SATISFYING WORK The research is clear. If you dislike your job, you will not enjoy a happy life. Of course, there are two solutions to this dilemma. The obvious one is to change jobs. A study by Henderson, Argyle and Furnham showed that getting a new job is likely to be one of life's most positive experiences. (We know this, and yet some of us choose to work for years in a job we hate rather than spending a little time finding a new one.)

The second solution is to change your attitude towards your job. Ask yourself, 'What is good about this job? How could I make it better? How could I design my work so that I could enjoy it?' After all, as Virgil said, 'There is nothing good or bad, but thinking makes it so.' A genuine change in attitude can often make a boring job fun again and reignite a career.

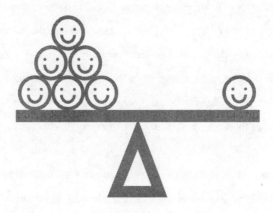

Time alone and with others

must be balanced

LIMIT TIME ALONE Some people love to be around others all the time; other people prefer to have more time to themselves. Follow your heart in this area, but be careful not to spend too much time alone. Several research studies suggest that people who spend a lot of their time alone experience higher than average rates of depression. Single people and introverts, for example, tend to be less happy.

Everyone needs a balance. But whenever you are uncertain whether you should see friends or not, it's probably a good idea to be social – if only for the sake of your wellbeing.

A plan helps you

hit your target

PLAN AND PRIORITISE   Ever heard the saying, 'Failing to plan is planning to fail'? Unfortunately most people go through life just playing it as it comes, with little planning. While this might appear to make things easier, it can lead to many more down periods. The brain loves order, and progress makes us feel good inside. Planning also increases our sense of control, a crucial factor in happiness.

Plan what you would like to achieve in your life, and refer to those plans regularly. (I know one highly successful real-estate agent who reads his life plan four times daily!) Create a 'To Do' list each day, and work through it. This will help give your brain the kind of ordered consciousness it craves.

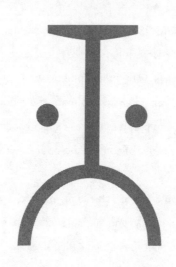

Alcohol is a depressant

REDUCE ALCOHOL   While alcohol appears to be a stimulant, it actually works as a depressant. Alcohol also plays havoc with the body's blood sugar levels, adversely affecting our mood for several days after consumption. If that's not bad enough, regular over-consumption of alcohol slowly poisons the kidneys and impedes brain functioning.

I'm not suggesting you don't touch a drop of alcohol (in fact, several studies show a daily glass of red wine is beneficial) but I am urging you to drink less than the average person if you want to keep your mood happy and stable.

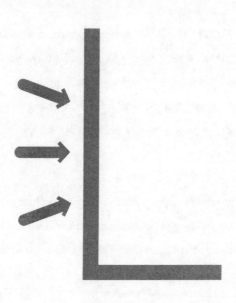

L-tyrosine defends
against depression

TAKE L-TYROSINE   L-tyrosine is an amino acid you can take to keep your mood up and your mind serene. The US Army discovered that L-tyrosine was able to ward off depression and many of the effects of stress amongst the soldiers it tested.

It's easy to find sources of L-tyrosine: chicken, turkey and most types of seafood are best. If you're vegetarian, don't worry – you can get ample amounts of L-tyrosine from tofu, beans, peas and lentils. Or ask at your local health-food shop for an amino acid supplement that contains L-tyrosine.

Music has a high
happiness success rate

LISTEN TO UPBEAT MUSIC   If you need a boost, music can have a quick and powerful impact on your mood. In fact, playing uplifting music has an 83% success rate in making people feel happier.

Why not create your own happy music collection? Gather 10 CDs that always make you feel good and keep them apart from the rest, ready for use when you're feeling low. Or better still, create your own tapes or CDs of inspiring music – your personal Happiness Hits!

I always do my
affirmations

I always do my
affirmations

I always do my
affirmations

I always do my
affirmations

USE POSITIVE AFFIRMATIONS Results show that 67% of people can improve their mood using this method. Simply write out a list of positive affirmations about how you would like to feel now. For example:

- 'I feel great.'
- 'I am always happy and relaxed.'
- 'I am loving to everyone.'
- 'I love life.'
- 'It's terrific to be alive.'

Then repeat these affirmations to yourself, each morning and evening, with passion. You'll be amazed at the difference this simple technique can make to the way you face each day.

Telling someone you care
makes both of you happier

EXPRESS YOUR LOVE Telling someone how much you love them is usually going to make them feel pretty fantastic. 'Being told I'm loved' ranked in the top 10 most pleasant activities by subjects in a recent research study.

But interestingly, it also works the other way. Wellbeing researchers Lewinsohn and Graf have shown that expressing our love for someone makes us feel good too. What's more, that feeling tends to stay with us the whole day.

In the hustle and bustle of our daily lives, it's easy to forget to take the time to show our love for those we care for. Ask yourself, 'Who are the five people in the world I care about most, and when was the last time I sat down and told them?'

people

Meeting new people
is an uplifting part of life

MEET NEW PEOPLE It's a fact that people's moods improve when they meet new people. It's easy to get into a social rut and only hang out with the same old friends. Yet weren't these great old friends once new acquaintances?

The truth is there are probably hundreds of people in your area who could become great pals, if only you took the time to meet them. Join a club, take up a hobby, attend a new social event each week. Creating regular opportunities to meet new people isn't just fun, it will inevitably lead to one or two new lifelong friends.

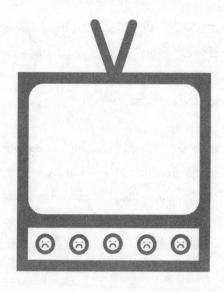

Watching TV

can make you sad

TURN OFF THE TV   Here's a weird fact: the average person now watches over four hours of television each day, yet research clearly shows it doesn't make us feel any better. In fact, the most common reported emotion while watching the box is mild depression.

It gets worse: a recent study showed that watching a lot of TV vastly increases our craving for more possessions, and every hour we watch reduces our contentment by around 5%.

It's time we turned off the box. First, make a pact with your family to have the TV on only three nights a week. Then work on reducing your viewing time even further over the next six months.

Volunteering lifts your mood

VOLUNTEER   We've all experienced that warm feeling inside when we do a favour for a friend or reach out to a stranger in need. Doing things for others makes us happy. And, not surprisingly, the more regularly we do something for someone else, the better we feel.

That's why volunteering for weekly community work is such a good idea. Whether it's helping out at an old people's home or lending a hand at the local school, volunteers feel – on average – two times happier with themselves than non-volunteers.

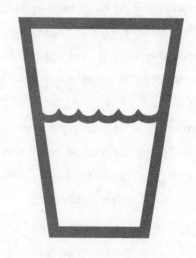

Half-empty
or half-full?

CHOOSE THE BRIGHT SIDE   The world is full of people who have had lots of good experiences in life, and yet they feel lousy. Then there are countless others who have faced overwhelming hardships, but they're bouncing along happily. Why?

Well, it's not the events in our lives that make us happy or sad, but our perception of what those events mean. By choosing to look on the good side of any hardship (and there is *always* something good), and electing to believe in ourselves and our ability to conquer or recover, there really is nothing that can get us down permanently.

Happy or sad – in the end, you choose.

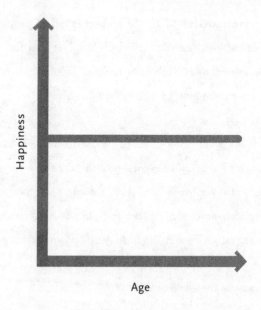

LOOK FORWARD TO THE FUTURE Many people fear getting old more than just about anything else. Perhaps that's because their vision of an old person's life is one of sickness, loneliness and misery. But research by Robert Kahn, professor of psychology and public health at the University of Michigan, shows that nothing could be further from the truth.

Old people are just as happy as young people. Kahn's work conclusively shows that age is completely unrelated to happiness. Many old people confirm that their senior years really are the 'golden years'. So don't even think about worrying. There are plenty of good times still ahead . . .

Regular conversations
make you feel better

HAVE MORE CONVERSATIONS People often report that they feel great after a good ol' chinwag. For centuries, a lively conversation about a subject that intrigues has proven as good a way as any to lift mood, and modern psychological studies confirm that most of us love to chat.

Why not set a goal to have at least one really good conversation each day? Ring a friend, approach someone at your office or simply engage with any of the people who cross your path daily. It only takes 20 minutes, but it can lift your mood for the rest of the day.

sexcellent

Feeling sexy has
excellent mental benefits

DRESS SEXILY   Here's an interesting piece of research. A study by Lewinsohn and Graf, wellbeing researchers, showed that being recognised by another as sexually attractive enhances our mood considerably. And what's more, we feel more positive for the whole day. We certainly love to be appreciated!

So don't leave it to chance. When appropriate, take the time to make yourself look good – even sexy – and you'll enjoy the mental benefits. By the way, that study also highlighted the importance of telling someone else when you find them attractive. In the right circumstances, of course.

holidays

Booking holidays in advance
doubles their pleasure

BOOK HOLIDAYS IN ADVANCE   Everyone loves holidays. The variety, the excitement and the relaxation all make taking a holiday one of life's most enjoyable events. But, like many things in life, the anticipation can be just as enjoyable as the event itself.

So it makes a lot of sense to plan your holidays well in advance. Planning induces pleasure in two ways:

1. Each time you get the brochures out or study the travel guides, you will get a rush of pleasure and excitement.
2. The fact that you've got a fantastic holiday booked for the future makes any hardship you're experiencing now just that bit more bearable.

You can't go past a pet

GET A PET Having a fluffy, friendly pal around the home does wonders for happiness. Most people report a considerable lift in mood when there's a pooch or kitty in their life. Indeed, in a major study, students rated getting a pet as one of the greatest positive events in their lives.

Your landlord won't allow a pet? No problem. Go down to the park in the mornings and give other people's pets a pat. It's almost impossible not to be uplifted when you give affection to animals, whether they're yours or someone else's.

The more activities,
often the more happiness

CREATE AN ACTIVITY GROUP As we've seen, hanging around with friends comprehensively increases happiness in most people. Almost every activity is enjoyed more when friends are about.

Why not organise an activity group to make social leisure activities more regular? In his brilliant book *The Psychology of Happiness*, Michael Argyle shows how much activity groups can enhance the wellbeing of everyone involved.

Here's how it might work. Put together a list of five or six people you enjoy being with and who you feel would get on with each other. Introduce the concept of the activity group and get each person to commit to coming up with one novel activity every month or so. That way, you'll have at least one enjoyable event to look forward to every week. Over a year, that adds up to a huge increase in fun!

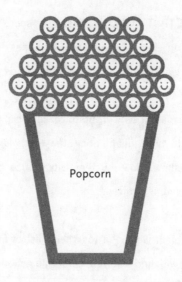

Popcorn

Watching films
is uplifting

BE A FILMGOER Watching uplifting films isn't just great fun, it can dramatically alter our mood. Several studies have shown that watching funny and inspirational films is one of the most effective methods of temporarily improving our spirits. A good technique is to schedule one specific night each week to go to the cinema. That way, you change film-watching from being an occasional pleasure to being a regular and powerful mood-lifter.

Even better, ask four or five friends to join you in creating a 'film club' and accompanying you each week. But remember – don't see anything depressing or violent. Those kinds of films often leave us with feelings opposite to the ones we want.

smooch

Kissing feels great

KISS SOMEONE We all like a good smooch. Maybe because a kiss is a form of affectionate interaction with another person, maybe because we like how it feels, maybe simply because it indicates that someone really likes us. (In some cases, really *really* likes us!) Whatever the reason, science backs up what most of us intuitively feel – that kissing makes us feel happier.

So, are you kissing your partner enough? Could you arrange more kissing moments? It's definitely worth thinking about. Or if you're single, maybe it's worth relaxing your love rules a little, and getting some more smooch action. However you manage it, remember that kissing may be a simple thing – but it can have a truly wonderful effect on your smile-o-meter.

Cheering for a team

increases happiness by 4%

FOLLOW A TEAM   One way to get happier is to start barracking for your local sports team. A study by professors Shank and Beasley showed that those who follow a sports team are, on average, 4% happier. The study found that the sense of community a fan feels among other fans is a major part of the pleasant feeling that sports-goers experience.

This is coupled with the intense high that a hard-fought sports contest creates. Let's face it – there's nothing more exciting than your team getting home after a close battle with the top rival! So get out the local paper, find a team to support and book a couple of tickets for this weekend.

:(

Signals of unhappiness

can be very small

BE SENSITIVE   Most of us are busy these days and many of us are stressed. It's no surprise that sometimes we aren't particularly sensitive to the feelings of those around us. Our loved ones might indicate their dissatisfaction in subtle ways: a pause, a frown, a sigh, a different tone of voice. If we're not careful, we can ignore these signals of growing unhappiness and, over time, they can snowball into a genuine relationship rift.

A fascinating study recently showed that married couples who displayed sensitivity in communication rated their satisfaction with life around 17% higher than those who didn't. So, think for a moment. Could you have been missing some subtle signals of dissatisfaction from those you care about?

It is important
to study happiness

FOCUS ON HAPPINESS Perhaps the most important technique I have saved until last. If you genuinely want to have a high level of happiness in your life, it is crucial that you focus on your happiness every day. You must decide to be happy now, not some time in the future.

Happiness cannot be left on the backburner for when you have some spare time, or when you're feeling down. Happiness is both an art and a science, and deserves regular study and fine-tuning.

You now have access to numerous techniques that have been proven to increase your levels of joy and wellbeing. Use them. Become an expert at applying them. Make them a part of you. If you do, a happier life is assured.

RECOMMENDED READING

Baker, Dan & Stauth, Cameron, *What Happy People Know*, Rodale, New York, 2003.

Beck, Martha, *The Joy Diet*, Crown, New York, 2003.

Benson, Herbert, *The Relaxation Response*, HarperCollins, New York, 2000.

Csikszentmihalyi, Mihali, *Flow: The Psychology of Optimal Experience*, HarperCollins, New York, 1990.

Dwoskin, Hale & Canfield, Jack, *The Sedona Method*, Sedona, 2003.

H.H. Dalai Lama & Cutler, Harold, *The Art of Happiness*, Hodder Headline Australia, Sydney, 1998.

Myers, David, *The Pursuit of Happiness*, Avon Books, New York, 1992.

Niven, David, *The 100 Simple Secrets of Happy People*, Harper San Francisco, San Francisco, 2000.

Null, Gary, *The Food-Mood-Body Connection*, Seven Stories Press, New York, 2002.

Seligman, Martin *Authentic Happiness*, Free Press, New York, 2002.

Thayer, Robert, *Calm Energy*, Oxford University Press, New York, 2001.